D1555093

Make Your Own Ice Cream

Classic Recipes for Ice Cream, Sorbet, Italian Ice, Sherbet and Other Frozen Desserts

Sarah Tyson Rorer

DOVER PUBLICATIONS, INC.
Mineola, New York

Publisher's Note

The instructions were written for an old-fashioned ice cream maker, but the recipes themselves can be used with any modern-day ice cream maker as well.

Bibliographical Note

This Dover edition, first published in 2018, contains the frozen desserts section from *Mrs. Rorer's Ice Creams, Water Ices, Frozen Puddings Together with Refreshments for All Social Affairs*, published by Arnold and Company, Philadelphia, in 1913. Some of the original recipes have been altered slightly to reflect current terminology, and footnotes have been added to this edition for clarification.

Library of Congress Cataloging-in-Publication Data

Names: Rorer, S. T., 1849–1937, author.
Title: Make your own ice cream : classic recipes for ice cream, sorbet, Italian ice, sherbet and other frozen desserts / Sarah Tyson Rorer.
Other titles: Ice creams, water ices, frozen puddings, together with refreshments for all social affairs
Description: Dover edition. | Mineola, New York : Dover Publications, 2018. | Reprint of: Ice creams, water ices, frozen puddings, together with refreshments for all social affairs.—Philadelphia : Arnold and Company, 1913. Identifiers: LCCN 2017052317| ISBN 9780486822174 (paper back) | ISBN 0486822176 (paperback)
Subjects: LCSH: Ice cream, ices, etc. | BISAC: COOKING / Courses & Dishes / Desserts. | COOKING / Specific Ingredients / Dairy. | COOKING / Specific Ingredients / Fruit. | LCGFT: Cookbooks.
Classification: LCC TX795 .R6 2018 | DDC 641.86/2—dc23
LC record available at https://lccn.loc.gov/2017052317

Manufactured in the United States by LSC Communications
82217601   2018
www.doverpublications.com

CONTENTS

Foreword

CONTAINING GENERAL DIRECTIONS
FOR ALL RECIPES

In this book, Philadelphia Ice Creams, comprising the first group, are very palatable, but expensive. In many parts of the country it is quite difficult to get good cream. For that reason, I have given a group of creams, using part milk and part cream, but it must be remembered that it takes smart "juggling" to make ice cream from milk. By far better use condensed milk, with enough water or milk to rinse out the cans.

Ordinary fruit creams may be made with condensed milk, which, of course, is cheaper than ordinary milk and cream.

In places where neither cream nor condensed milk can be purchased, a fair ice cream is made by adding two tablespoons of olive oil to each quart of milk. The cream for Philadelphia Ice Cream should be rather rich, but not double cream.

If pure raw cream is stirred rapidly, it swells and becomes frothy, like the beaten whites of eggs, and is "whipped cream." To prevent this in making Philadelphia Ice Cream, one-half of the cream is scalded, and when it is very cold, the remaining half of raw cream is added. This gives the smooth, light, and rich consistency which makes these creams so different from others.

USE OF FRUITS

Use fresh fruits in the summer and the best canned unsweetened fruits in the winter. If sweetened fruits must be used, cut down the given quantity of sugar. Where acidic fruits are used, they should be added to the cream after it is partly frozen.

TIME FOR FREEZING

The time for freezing varies according to the quality of cream or milk or water; water ices require a longer time than ice creams.* It is not advised to freeze the mixtures too rapidly; they are apt to be coarse, not smooth; and if they are churned before the mixture is icy cold, they will be greasy or "buttery."

The average time for freezing two quarts of cream should be ten minutes; it takes but a minute or two longer for larger quantities.

DIRECTIONS FOR FREEZING

Pound the ice in a large bag with a mallet, or use an ordinary ice shaver. The finer the ice, the less time it takes to freeze the cream. A four-quart freezer will require ten pounds of ice, and a quart and a pint of coarse rock salt. You may pack the freezer with a layer of ice three inches thick, then a layer of salt one inch thick, or mix the ice and salt in the tub and shovel it around the freezer. Before beginning to pack the freezer, turn the crank to see that all the machinery is in working order. Then open the can and turn in the mixture that is to be frozen. Turn the crank slowly and steadily until the mixture begins to freeze, then more rapidly until it is completely frozen. If the freezer is properly packed, it will take fifteen minutes to freeze the mixture. Philadelphia Ice Creams are not good if frozen too quickly.

TO REPACK

After the cream is frozen, wipe off the lid of the can and remove the crank; take off the lid, being very careful not to allow any salt to fall into the can. Remove the dasher and scrape it off. Take a large knife or steel spatula, scrape the cream from the sides of the can, and work and pack it down until it is perfectly smooth. Put the lid back on the can, and put a cork in the hole from which the dasher was taken. Draw off the water, repack, and cover the whole with a piece of brown paper; throw over a heavy bag or a bit of burlap, and let stand for one or two hours to ripen.

---

* See more detailed directions for water ices on page 60.

TO MOLD ICE CREAMS, ICES OR PUDDINGS

If you wish to pack ice cream and serve it in forms or shapes, it must be molded after the freezing. The handiest of all of these molds is either the brick or the melon mold.*

After the cream is frozen rather stiff, prepare a tub or bucket of coarsely chopped ice, with one-half less salt than you use for freezing. To each ten pounds of ice, allow one quart of rock salt. Sprinkle a little rock salt in the bottom of your bucket or tub, then put over a layer of cracked ice, another layer of salt and cracked ice, and on this place your mold, which is not filled, but is covered with a lid, and pack it all around, leaving the top, of course, to pack later on. Take your freezer near this tub. Remove the lid from the mold, and pack in the cream, smoothing it down until you have filled it to overflowing. Smooth the top with a spatula or limber knife, cover with a sheet of waxed paper, and adjust the lid. Have a strip of muslin or cheesecloth dipped in hot paraffin to quickly bind the seam of the lid. This will remove all danger of salt water entering the pudding. Now cover the mold thoroughly with ice and salt.

Make sure that your packing tub or bucket has a hole below the top of the mold, so that the salt water will be drained off.

If you are packing in small molds, each mold, as fast as it is closed, should be wrapped in wax paper and put down into the salt and ice. These must be filled quickly and packed.

Molds should stand two hours or longer.

TO REMOVE ICE CREAMS, ICES AND PUDDINGS FROM MOLDS

Ice cream may be molded in the freezer; you will then have a perfectly round smooth mold, which serves very well for puddings that are to be garnished, and saves a great deal of trouble and extra expense for salt and ice.

---

* Many of these vintage molds have today been replaced with stainless steel or silicone molds.

As cold water is warmer than the ordinary freezing mixture, after you lift the can or mold, wipe off the salt, hold it for a minute under cold water, then quickly wipe the top and bottom and remove the lid. Loosen the pudding with a limber knife, hold the mold a little slanted, give it a shake, and nine times out of ten it will come out quickly, having the perfect shape of the can or mold. If the cream still sticks and refuses to come out, wipe the mold with a towel soaked in warm water. Hot water spoils the gloss of puddings, and unless you know exactly how to use it, the cream will be too melted to garnish.

All frozen puddings, water ices, sherbets, and sorbets are frozen and molded according to these directions.

QUANTITIES FOR SERVING

The quantities given in these recipes are arranged in equal amounts so that for a smaller number of people they can be easily divided. Each quart of ice cream will serve, in dessert plates, four people. In stem ice cream dishes, silver or glass, it will serve six people. A quart of ice cream or sherbet will fill ten small sherbet stem glasses, to serve with the main course at dinner. In lemonade glasses, this quantity will serve eight people.

Philadelphia
Ice Creams

APPLE ICE CREAM

- ❋ 4 large tart apples
- ❋ 1 quart of cream
- ❋ ½ pound of sugar
- ❋ 1 tablespoon of lemon juice

Put half the cream and all the sugar over the heat and stir until the sugar is dissolved. When the mixture is perfectly cold, freeze it and add the lemon juice and the apples, pared and grated. Finish the freezing, and repack to ripen.

The apples must be pared at the last minute and grated into the cream. If they are grated on a dish and allowed to remain in the air, they will turn very dark and spoil the color of the cream.

BANANA ICE CREAM

- ❋ 1 quart of cream
- ❋ 6 large bananas
- ❋ ½ pound of sugar
- ❋ 1 teaspoon of vanilla extract

Put half the cream and all the sugar over the heat and stir until the sugar is dissolved. Remove from the heat, and, when perfectly cold, add the remaining half of the cream. Freeze the mixture, and add the bananas, which have been mashed or pressed through a colander. Put on the lid, adjust the crank, and turn until the mixture is frozen rather hard.

This will serve ten people.

APRICOT ICE CREAM

* ✳ 6 ounces of sugar
* ✳ 1 quart of cream
* ✳ 1 can of apricots or
* ✳ 1 quart of fresh apricots (add 4 additional ounces of sugar)

If fresh apricots are used, add an extra quarter pound of sugar (4 ounces). Put half the cream and all the sugar over the heat in a double boiler and stir until the sugar is dissolved; remove from the heat and, when cold, add the remaining cream. Place the mixture into the freezer, and, when frozen fairly stiff, add the apricots (after they have been pressed through a colander). Return the lid, adjust the crank, and turn it slowly for five minutes, then remove the dasher and repack.

This will serve ten people.

BISCOTTI ICE CREAM

* ✳ 6 biscotti
* ✳ 1 quart of cream
* ✳ ½ pound of sugar
* ✳ 1 teaspoon of vanilla extract

Grate and sift the biscotti. Scald half the cream and the sugar; when cold, add the remaining cream and the vanilla extract, and freeze. When frozen, remove the dasher, stir in the powdered biscotti, and repack to ripen.

This will serve six people.

BISQUE ICE CREAM

* 1 quart of cream
* ¼ pound of almond macaroons
* 4 chocolate kisses
* ½ pound of sugar
* 1 slice of stale sponge cake or
* 2 stale ladyfingers
* 1 teaspoon of caramel
* 1 teaspoon of vanilla extract
* 4 tablespoons of sherry

Pound the macaroons, kisses, ladyfingers or sponge cake, and put them through a colander. Put half the cream and all the sugar over the heat in a double boiler; when the sugar is dissolved, stand the mixture aside to cool; when cold, add the remaining cream, caramel, sherry, and vanilla extract.

Put the mixture into the freezer, and, when frozen, add the pounded cakes; stir the mixture until it is perfectly smooth and well mixed, and repack.

Bisque ice cream is best when it stands for three hours.

This will serve six people.

BROWN BREAD ICE CREAM

* 3 half-inch slices of Boston Brown Bread
* 1 quart of cream
* ½ pound of sugar
* ¼ of a vanilla bean or 1 teaspoon of vanilla extract

Dry and toast the bread in the oven, grate or pound it, and put it through an ordinary sieve. Heat half the cream and all the sugar; remove from the heat, add vanilla, and, when cold, add the remaining cream, and freeze. When frozen, remove the dasher, stir in the brown bread, repack, and let stand to ripen.

This will serve six people.

BURNT ALMOND ICE CREAM

* 1 quart of cream
* ½ pound of sugar
* 4 ounces of sweet almonds
* 1 tablespoon of caramel
* 1 teaspoon of vanilla extract
* 4 tablespoons of sherry

Shell, blanch and roast the almonds until they are a golden brown, then grate them. Put half the cream and all the sugar over the heat in a double boiler. Stir until the sugar is dissolved; remove from the heat, add the caramel and the almonds, and, when cold, add the remaining pint of cream, the vanilla extract, and the sherry. Freeze.

This will serve eight people.

CHOCOLATE ICE CREAM

* ❋ 1 quart of cream
* ❋ 1 pint of milk
* ❋ ½ pound of sugar
* ❋ 4 ounces of chocolate
* ❋ ¼ of a vanilla bean or 1 teaspoon of vanilla extract
* ❋ ¼ teaspoon of cinnamon

Grate the chocolate, put it in a double boiler with the milk; stir until hot, and add the sugar, vanilla, cinnamon, and one pint of the cream. When cold, freeze; when frozen, remove the dasher and stir in the remaining pint of the cream whipped to a stiff froth.

This will serve ten people.

CARAMEL ICE CREAM, NO. 1

* ❋ 1 quart of cream
* ❋ ½ pound of sugar
* ❋ 1 teaspoon of vanilla extract

Put four tablespoons of the sugar in an iron frying pan over a strong heat, shake until the sugar melts, turns brown, smokes, and burns; add quickly a half cup of water; let it boil a minute; remove from the heat, and put it, with all the sugar and half the cream, in a double boiler over the heat. Stir until the sugar is dissolved; remove from the heat, and, when cold, add the remaining cream and vanilla extract, and freeze.

This will serve six people.

CARAMEL ICE CREAM, NO. 2

* ❊ 1 quart of cream
* ❊ 1 pint of milk
* ❊ ½ cup of brown sugar
* ❊ ½ pound of granulated sugar
* ❊ 2 teaspoons of vanilla extract

Put the brown sugar in a frying pan over the heat, shake it until it melts, burns, and smokes. Remove from the heat and add two tablespoons of water; heat until the sugar is again melted, put it in a double boiler with the milk and all the sugar, stir until the sugar is dissolved, and let it cool. When cold, add half the cream and the vanilla extract, and freeze.

When frozen sufficiently stiff to remove the dasher, stir in the remaining pint of cream whipped to a stiff froth, repack, and let stand for three hours.

This will serve ten people.

COFFEE ICE CREAM

* ❊ 1 quart of cream
* ❊ ½ pound of powdered sugar
* ❊ 4 ounces of Mocha Java coffee beans

Grind the Mocha Java rather coarse, put it in the double boiler with one half the cream, and steep over the heat for at least ten minutes. Strain through a fine muslin bag, pressing it hard to get out all the strength of the coffee. Add the sugar and stir until dissolved; when cold, add the remaining pint of cream and freeze.

This will serve six people.

CURAÇAO ICE CREAM

* 1 quart of cream
* 1 tablespoon of curaçao
* ½ pound of sugar
* 2 tablespoons of orange blossom water
* Juice of 2 oranges

Put the sugar and half the cream over the heat in a double boiler. When the sugar is dissolved, remove from the heat, and, when cold, add the curaçao, orange juice, and orange blossom water; add the remaining cream, and freeze.

This will serve six people.

GINGER ICE CREAM

* 1 quart of cream
* ¼ pound of crystallized ginger
* ½ pound of sugar
* 1 tablespoon of lemon juice

Put the ginger through an ordinary food chopper. Heat the sugar, ginger, and half the cream in a double boiler; when the sugar is dissolved, remove it from the heat, and, when cold, add the lemon juice and remaining cream, and freeze.

GREEN GAGE ICE CREAM

- ✳ 1 quart of cream
- ✳ 4 ounces of sugar
- ✳ 1 pint of preserved green gage plums, free from syrup

Press the green gage plums through a sieve. Add the sugar to half the cream, stir it in a double boiler until the sugar is dissolved; when cold, add the remaining cream. When this is partly frozen, stir in the green gage pulp, and finish the freezing as directed on page vi.

If the green gage plums are colorless, add three or four drops of green food coloring to the cream before freezing.

LEMON ICE CREAM

- ✳ 1 quart of cream
- ✳ 9 ounces of powdered sugar
- ✳ Grated yellow rind of 3 lemons
- ✳ 4 tablespoons of juice from lemons
- ✳ Juice of one orange

Mix the sugar, the grated rind and juice of the lemons, and the juice from the orange together. Put half the cream in a double boiler over the heat; when scalding hot, stand it aside until perfectly cold; add the remaining half of the cream, and freeze it rather hard. Remove the crank and the lid, add the sugar mixture, replace the lid and crank, and turn rapidly for five minutes; repack to ripen.

This will serve six people.

MARASCHINO ICE CREAM

* 1 quart of cream
* ½ pound of sugar
* 1 orange
* 2 tablespoons of maraschino*
* 2 drops of Angostura Bitters, or
* ½ teaspoon of wild cherry extract

Put the sugar and half the cream in a double boiler, and stir until the sugar is dissolved. When cold, add the remaining cream, the juice of the orange, the bitters or wild cherry extract, and the maraschino, and freeze.

Using parfait glasses, this will serve six people.

ORANGE ICE CREAM

* 1 quart of cream
* 10 ounces of sugar
* Juice of 6 large oranges
* Grated rind of one orange

Put the sugar, grated rind of the orange, and half the cream in a double boiler over the heat; when the sugar is dissolved, remove from the heat, and, when very cold, add the remaining cream, and freeze. When frozen rather hard, add the orange juice, refreeze, and pack to ripen.

---

*Maraschino here refers to maraschino liqueur. Grenadine syrup may be used in place of maraschino.

PINEAPPLE ICE CREAM

- ❉ 1 quart of cream
- ❉ 12 ounces of sugar
- ❉ 1 large ripe pineapple or
- ❉ 1 pint can (16 oz.) of chopped pineapple
- ❉ Juice of one lemon

Put half the cream and half the sugar in a double boiler over the heat; when the sugar is dissolved, stand it aside until cold. Pare and grate the pineapple, add the remaining half of the sugar, and stand it aside. When the cream is cold, add the remaining cream, and partly freeze. Then add the lemon juice to the pineapple and add it to the frozen cream; turn the freezer five minutes longer, and repack.

This will serve eight or ten people.

PISTACHIO ICE CREAM

- ❉ 1 quart of cream
- ❉ ½ pound of sugar
- ❉ ½ pound of shelled pistachio nuts
- ❉ 1 teaspoon of almond extract
- ❉ 10 drops of green food coloring

Blanch and pound or grate the nuts. Put half the cream and all the sugar in a double boiler; stir until the sugar is dissolved and let stand to cool. When cold, add the nuts, the flavoring, and the remaining cream; mix, add the food coloring, and turn into the freezer.

This will serve six people.

RASPBERRY ICE CREAM

* ⁕ 1 quart of cream
* ⁕ 1 quart of raspberries
* ⁕ 12 ounces of sugar
* ⁕ Juice of one lemon

Mash the raspberries; add half the sugar and the lemon juice. Put the remaining sugar and half the cream in a double boiler; stir until the sugar is dissolved, and let stand to cool; when cold, add the remaining cream, turn the mixture into the freezer, and stir until partly frozen. Remove the lid and add the mashed raspberries, and stir again for five or ten minutes until the mixture is sufficiently hard to repack.

This will serve eight or ten people.

STRAWBERRY ICE CREAM

Make precisely the same as for the raspberry ice cream, substituting one quart of strawberries for the raspberries.

VANILLA ICE CREAM

* 1 quart of cream
* ½ pound of sugar
* 1 vanilla bean or
* 2 teaspoons of vanilla extract

Put the sugar and half the cream in a double boiler over the heat. Split the vanilla bean, scrape out the seeds and add them to the hot cream, and add the bean broken into pieces. Stir until the sugar is dissolved, and strain through a colander. When this is cold, add the remaining cream and freeze. This should be repacked and given two to four hours to ripen.

This will serve six people.

WALNUT ICE CREAM

* 1 quart of cream
* ½ pound of sugar
* 1 teaspoon of vanilla extract
* 1 teaspoon of caramel extract
* ½ pint of black walnut meat

Put the sugar and half the cream over the heat in a double boiler; when the sugar is dissolved, let it stand to cool. When cold, add the remaining cream, the chopped walnuts, and the vanilla and caramel extracts, and freeze.

This will serve six people.

Neapolitan Creams

In this group we have a set of frozen desserts called by many "ice creams," but which are really flavored frozen custards. In localities where cream is not accessible, the Neapolitan Creams are far better than milk thickened with cornstarch or gelatin.

CARAMEL

* ❊ 1 pint of cream
* ❊ 1 pint of milk
* ❊ ½ pound of sugar
* ❊ 4 eggs
* ❊ 3 tablespoons of caramel
* ❊ 1 teaspoon of vanilla extract

Beat the yolks of the eggs until creamy and add the sugar; beat until light, and then add the well-beaten whites of the eggs. Put the milk over the heat in a double boiler; when hot, add the eggs, and stir and cook until the mixture begins to thicken. Remove from the heat, strain through a fine sieve, add the vanilla extract and caramel, and, when cold, add the cream, and freeze.

This will serve ten people.

COFFEE

* ❊ 1 pint of strong black coffee
* ❊ 1 pint of cream
* ❊ 2 eggs
* ❊ ½ pound of sugar
* ❊ 1 teaspoon of vanilla extract

Beat the sugar and the yolks of the eggs until light, add the well-beaten whites, and pour them into the coffee, boiling hot. Stir over the heat for a minute. Remove from the heat, add the vanilla extract, and, when cold, add the cream, and freeze.

This will serve eight people.

CHOCOLATE

* 1 pint of cream
* 1 pint of milk
* ½ pound of sugar
* 4 eggs
* 2 ounces of chocolate, grated
* 1 small piece of stick cinnamon
* 1 teaspoon of vanilla extract

Put the milk and cinnamon over the heat in a double boiler. Beat the yolks of the eggs and sugar until very light, add the well-beaten whites, and stir this into the hot milk. As soon as the mixture begins to thicken, remove it from the heat, add the grated chocolate, and, when cold, add the cream and the vanilla extract. Freeze and pack as directed on page vi.

This will serve ten people.

NEAPOLITAN BLOCKS

These are made by putting layers of various kinds and colors of ice creams into a brick mold.* Pack and freeze. At serving time, cut into slices crosswise of the brick, and serve each slice on a paper mat.

---

* Any square or rectangular mold may be used to make the "brick" or "block" in layers of different flavors and colors. Silicone and stainless steel molds may be substituted.

VANILLA

* ❋ 1 pint of cream
* ❋ 1 pint of milk
* ❋ ½ pound of sugar
* ❋ 3 eggs
* ❋ ¼ of a vanilla bean or 1 teaspoon of vanilla extract

Put the milk over the heat in a double boiler, and add the split vanilla bean or vanilla extract. Beat the yolks of the eggs and the sugar until light; add the whites beaten to a stiff froth, and stir the hot milk into them. Return the mixture to the double boiler and cook until it begins to thicken, or until it coats a knife blade dipped into it. Remove from the heat, strain through a colander, and, when cold, add the cream, and freeze. Repack and let stand to ripen for three hours or longer.

This will serve eight people.

WALNUT

* ❊ 1 pint of cream
* ❊ 1 pint of milk
* ❊ 2 eggs
* ❊ ½ pint of chopped black walnuts
* ❊ 1 teaspoon of vanilla extract
* ❊ 1 teaspoon of caramel extract

Beat the yolks of the eggs and the sugar until light; add the well-beaten whites, and then the milk, scalding hot. Stir over the heat in a double boiler until the mixture begins to thicken. Remove from the heat, and add the vanilla extract and caramel. When cold, add the walnuts and cream, and freeze.

This will serve eight people.

Ice Creams from Condensed Milk

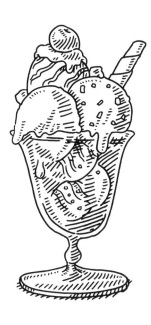

These creams are not as good as those made from raw cream, but with care and good flavoring are quite as good as the ordinary Neapolitan Creams. There is one advantage—condensed milk is not as liable to curdle when mixed with fresh fruits. These recipes will answer also for what is sold under the name of "Evaporated Cream." Use unsweetened milk, or allow for the sugar in the sweetened varieties.

BANANA

* ❋ 6 large bananas
* ❋ ¼ pound of sugar
* ❋ 1 half-pint can (8 oz.) of condensed milk
* ❋ ½ cup of water
* ❋ Juice of one lemon

Press the bananas through a sieve, and add the lemon juice and sugar. Set aside for a half hour, add milk and water, stir until the sugar is dissolved, and freeze as directed on page vi.

This will serve six people.

CARAMEL

* ❋ ¼ cup of brown sugar
* ❋ ½ cup of granulated sugar
* ❋ 1 cup of water
* ❋ 2 half-pint cans (16 oz. total) of condensed milk
* ❋ 1 teaspoon of vanilla extract

Put the brown sugar in an iron pan, melt and brown it. When it begins to smoke, add two tablespoons of hot water. Stir until liquid. Pour out the milk, rinse the cans with the water, add the caramel, vanilla extract, and granulated sugar. When the sugar is dissolved, freeze as directed on page vi.

This will serve six people.

CHOCOLATE, NO. 1

- ✳ 2 ounces of Baker's chocolate
- ✳ ½ pint of water
- ✳ ¼ teaspoon of ground cinnamon
- ✳ 2 half-pint cans (16 oz. total) of condensed milk
- ✳ 1 teaspoon of vanilla extract
- ✳ ¼ pound of sugar

Put the water, chocolate, sugar, and cinnamon in a saucepan; stir until boiling. Remove from the heat, add the vanilla extract, and the condensed milk. When cold, freeze as directed on page vi.

This will serve six people.

CHOCOLATE, NO. 2

- ✳ 4 ounces of Baker's chocolate
- ✳ ½ pint of water
- ✳ ½ pound of sugar
- ✳ 2 half-pint cans (16 oz. total) of condensed milk
- ✳ 1 pint of milk
- ✳ 2 teaspoons of vanilla extract
- ✳ ¼ teaspoon of ground cinnamon

Put the chocolate, sugar, water, and cinnamon in a saucepan over the heat. Stir until the mixture boils. Remove from the heat, and add all the remaining ingredients. When cold, freeze as directed on page vi.

This will serve eight people.

COCONUT

- ❋ 2 large coconuts
- ❋ 1 pint of boiling water
- ❋ 1 half-pint can (8 oz.) of sweetened condensed milk

Grate the coconuts and pour the boiling water over them. Stir until it is cool, and press in a sieve. Put the fiber in a cheese cloth and wring it dry; add this to the water that was strained through the sieve. When cold, add the sweetened condensed milk, and freeze as directed on page vi.

This will serve eight people.

COFFEE

- ❋ 1 pint of strong black coffee
- ❋ ½ cup of sugar
- ❋ 1 half-pint can (8 oz.) of condensed milk
- ❋ 1 teaspoon of vanilla extract

Add the sugar to the hot coffee, and stir until it is dissolved; add the milk, using water enough to rinse out the can; add the vanilla extract. When the mixture is cold, freeze, turning it rapidly toward the end of the freezing.

This will serve four people.

ORANGE, NO. 1

* ❊ 1 full pint of orange juice
* ❊ ⅔ cup of sugar
* ❊ 1 half-pint can (8 oz.) of condensed milk
* ❊ Grated rind of 2 oranges

Grate the rinds into the sugar, add milk and enough water to rinse the can. When sugar is dissolved, let stand in a cold place. Put orange juice in the freezer and freeze until quite hard; add the sweetened milk mixture, and freeze again quickly.

This will serve four people.

ORANGE, NO. 2

Freeze a full quart of orange juice. When quite hard, add a can of sweetened condensed milk, freeze it again, and serve at once.

This will serve eight people.

ORANGE GELATIN CREAM

* ½ pint of orange juice
* 1 package of orange gelatin
* ½ pound of sugar
* 1 pint (16 oz.) of unsweetened condensed milk
* ½ pint of water

Add the grated rind of two oranges to the gelatin; add the sugar and the boiling water. Stir until the sugar and gelatin are dissolved, add the orange juice, and when the mixture is cold, put it in the freezer and stir slowly until it begins to freeze. Add the condensed milk, and continue the freezing.

This is nice served in tall glasses, with the beaten whites of the eggs made into a meringue and heaped on top.

This will serve eight people.

SOURSOP

* 1 large soursop or cherimoya
* ¼ pound of sugar
* ½ pint can (8 oz.) of unsweetened condensed milk
* 4 tablespoons of boiling water
* Juice of one lime

Squeeze the soursop or cherimoya, which should measure nearly one quart; add the sugar melted in the water with the lime juice and milk, and freeze slowly.

This will serve ten people.

PEACH

- ❋ 12 ripe or canned peaches
- ❋ 4 peach kernels
- ❋ ½ pint of water
- ❋ 2 half-pint cans (16 oz. total) of unsweetened condensed milk
- ❋ ½ pound of sugar

Put the sugar, water, and peach kernels over the heat; stir until the sugar is dissolved, and boil three minutes. Pare the peaches and press them through a colander; add the strained syrup to the peaches. When cold, turn the mixture into the freezer and turn the crank slowly until partly frozen; add the milk, and continue the freezing.

If you are using canned peaches, omit the water and use less sugar.

This will serve ten people.

Frozen Puddings and Desserts

ALASKA BAKE

Make a vanilla ice cream, one or two quarts, as the occasion demands. When the ice cream is frozen, pack it in a brick mold*, cover each side of the mold with paper, and fasten the bottom and lid. Wrap the whole brick in wax paper, and pack it in salt and ice; freeze for at least two hours before serving time. At serving time, make a meringue from the whites of six eggs beaten to a froth; add six tablespoons of sifted powdered sugar, and beat until fine and dry. Turn the ice cream from the mold, place it on a serving platter, and stand the platter on a cutting board.

Cover the mold with the meringue pressed through a star tube in a pastry bag, or spread it all over the ice cream as you would ice a cake. Decorate the top quickly, and dust it thickly with powdered sugar; stand it under the gas burners in a gas broiler or on the grate in a hot coal or wood oven until it is lightly browned, and send it quickly to the table. There is no danger of the ice cream melting if you will protect the underside of the plate. The meringue acts as a nonconductor for the upper part.

A two-quart mold with meringue will serve ten people.

---

* Any square or rectangular mold may be used if a traditional brick mold is not available. A silicone or stainless steel mold may be substituted.

ALEXANDER BOMB

* 1 pint of cream
* 1 pint of milk
* 4 eggs
* 4 tart apples
* 1 pint of water
* 8 ounces of orange blossom water
* 1 tablespoon of curaçao
* 1 pound of sugar
* Juice of one lemon

Peel, core, and quarter the apples; put them in a saucepan with the grated rind of the lemon, half the sugar, and all the water; boil until tender, and add the juice of the lemon; rub the apples through a sieve.

When cold, freeze. Whip the cream. Beat the eggs and the remaining sugar and add them to the hot milk; stir until the mixture thickens. Remove from the heat, and, when cold, add the orange blossom water and the curaçao; freeze in another freezer. Divide the whipped cream, and stir one-half into the first and one-half into the other mixture. Line a melon mold with the custard mixture, fill the center space with the frozen apples, and cover over another layer of the custard; cover with a sheet of paper, and put on the lid. Bind the seam with a strip of muslin dipped in paraffin and pack the mold in salt and ice; freeze for at least two hours. Serve plain, or it may be garnished with whipped cream.

This will serve twelve people.

BISCUITS AMERICANA

* 1 quart of cream
* ½ pound of sugar
* ¼ pound of Jordan almonds
* 1 teaspoon of almond extract
* 1 teaspoon of vanilla extract
* Yolks of six eggs
* Grated rind of one lemon

Put half the cream in a double boiler over the heat, and, when hot, add the yolks of the eggs and sugar, beaten until very, very light; add all the flavoring, and let stand until very cold; when cold, freeze in an ordinary freezer. Whip the remaining pint of cream, add one-half of it to the frozen mixture, repack, and let stand to ripen. Blanch, dry, and chop the almonds. Put them in the oven and shake constantly until they are golden brown. At serving time, fill the frozen mixture quickly into paper dessert cups; with the remaining whipped cream in a pastry bag with star tube, make a little rosette on the top of each case, dust thickly with the chopped almonds, and send to the table.

This will fill twelve paper dessert cups of ordinary size.

BISCUITS GLACÉ

* 1 pint of cream
* ¾ pound of sugar
* 1 pint of water
* ½ cup of sherry
* 2 tablespoons of brandy
* 1 teaspoon of vanilla extract
* Yolks of six eggs

Put the sugar and water in a saucepan over the heat and stir until the sugar is dissolved; wipe down the sides of the pan, and boil until the syrup spins a heavy thread or makes a soft ball when dropped into cold water. Beat the yolks of the eggs to a cream, add them to the boiling syrup, and with an eggbeater whisk over the heat until you have a custard-like mixture that will thickly coat a knife blade; strain through a sieve into a bowl, and whisk until the mixture is stiff and cold. It should look like a very light sponge cake batter. Add the flavoring. Whip the cream and stir it carefully into the mixture. Fill the mixture into paper dessert cups or individual dishes, stand them in a freezing cave* or in a tin bucket that is well packed in salt and ice, cover and freeze for at least four or five hours.

At serving time, dust the tops of the biscuits with grated macaroons or chopped almonds, dish on paper mats, and send to the table.

This will fill fifteen biscuit cases.

---

* A freezer chest can be used as well.

BISCUITS À LA MARIE

* ½ pound of sugar
* 1 pint of water
* ½ pint of cream
* ½ pound of almond macaroons
* ¼ pound of candied or maraschino cherries
* 1 teaspoon of bitter almond extract
* Yolks of six eggs

Boil the sugar and water until the syrup is in the thread stage. Add the eggs, beaten until very light. Whip this over the heat for three minutes, remove from the heat, strain into a bowl, and whip until thick and cold.

Add the flavoring and the macaroons, which have been dried, grated, and sifted. Add the cream, whipped. Fill the mixture into paper dessert cups, and freeze as directed for Biscuits Glacé.

An extra half-pint of cream may be whipped for garnish at serving time, if desired; otherwise, garnish the top with chopped maraschino cherries, and send to the table.

This will fill twelve biscuit cases.

BISCUIT TORTONI

- ❊ 1 quart of cream
- ❊ ½ pound of sugar
- ❊ ½ cup of maraschino*
- ❊ 2 tablespoons of sherry
- ❊ 1 teaspoon of vanilla extract
- ❊ Yolks of six eggs

Put half the cream in a double boiler over the heat. Beat the sugar and yolks together until very, very light, add them to the hot cream and stir over the heat until the mixture begins to thicken. Remove from the heat, and, when very cold, add the vanilla extract, maraschino, and sherry, and freeze.

When frozen, stir in the remaining cream, whipped to a stiff froth. Fill individual dishes, stand at once in the ice cave (freezer chest or cooler), pack and freeze for three to four hours.

This will serve twelve people.

....

BOMB GLACÉ

Pack a two-quart bomb glacé (spherical—resembling a cannonball) mold in salt and ice. Remove the lid, and line the mold with a quart of well-made vanilla ice cream. Fill the center with one-half the recipe for Biscuit Glacé mixture, which has been packed in a freezer until icy cold. Put on the lid, bind the edge with a piece of muslin dipped in paraffin, cover the mold with salt and ice, and let stand three hours to freeze.

This will serve twelve people.

---

* Maraschino here refers to maraschino liqueur. Grenadine syrup may be used in place of maraschino.

CABINET PUDDING, ICED

* 1 quart of milk
* 6 eggs
* ¼ pound of powdered sugar
* 1 tablespoon of powdered gelatin
* ¼ pound of macaroons and ladyfingers, mixed
* ½ pound of conserved cherries or pineapple
* ½ pound of stale sponge cake
* 1 teaspoon of vanilla extract

Grate the macaroons and ladyfingers and rub them through a coarse sieve. Cut the sponge cake into slices and then into strips. Put the milk over the heat in a double boiler and add the eggs and sugar beaten together until light; stir and cook until the mixture is sufficiently thick to coat a knife blade. Remove from the heat, add the gelatin, strain, and let stand to cool. Garnish the bottom of a two-quart melon mold with the cherries or pineapple, put in a layer of the sponge cake, then a sprinkling of the macaroons and ladyfingers, another layer of the cherries, then the sponge cake, and continue until you have used all the ingredients. Add a teaspoon of vanilla extract to the custard, pour it in the mold, cover the mold with the lid, bind the seam with muslin dipped in paraffin, pack in salt and ice, and let stand for three hours.

At serving time, dip the mold quickly into hot water, wipe it off, remove the lid, and turn the pudding onto a cold platter. Drizzle Montrose Sauce (see recipe, page 93) on top.

This will serve ten to twelve people.

ICED CAKE

Make an Angel Food or a Sunshine Cake and bake it in a square mold. Make a plain frozen custard, and flavor it with vanilla extract; pack it and leave it until serving time. Cut off the top of the cake, take out the center, leaving a bottom and wall one inch thick. At serving time, fill the cake quickly with the frozen custard, replace the top, dust it thickly with powdered sugar and chopped almonds, and send it to the table with a sauceboat of cold Montrose Sauce (see recipe, page 93).

This cake may be varied by using different garnishes. Maraschino cherries may be used in place of almonds, or the base of the cake may be garnished with preserved green walnuts or green gage plums, or the top and sides may be garnished with rosettes of whipped cream.

This will serve twelve people.

QUICK CAFÉ PARFAIT

Make a quart of plain Coffee Ice Cream, freeze, and pack it. Whip one pint of cream. At serving time, stir the whipped cream into the frozen coffee cream, dish it at once into tall parfait glasses, garnish the top with a rosette of whipped cream, and send at once to the table.

This will fill eight glasses.

QUICK CARAMEL PARFAIT

Make a quart of Caramel Ice Cream, pack, and stand it aside for two hours. At serving time, stir in a pint of cream, whipped to a stiff froth, dish in parfait glasses, and send to the table. The top of the glasses may be garnished with whipped cream, if desired.

This will fill eight glasses.

QUICK STRAWBERRY PARFAIT

This is made precisely the same as other parfaits, with Strawberry Ice Cream, and whipped cream stirred in at serving time. Serve in parfait glasses, garnish the top with whipped cream, with a strawberry in the center on top.

This will fill eight glasses.

QUICK CHOCOLATE PARFAIT

Make one quart of Chocolate Ice Cream, and add one pint of whipped cream, according to the preceding recipes.

This will fill eight glasses.

BOSTON PUDDING

Make Boston Brown Bread Ice Cream and half the recipe for Tutti Frutti (see recipe, page 51). When both are frozen, line a melon mold with the Brown Bread Ice Cream, fill the center with the Tutti Frutti, cover over more of the Brown Bread Ice Cream, fasten tightly, and bind the seam of the lid with a strip of muslin dipped in paraffin. Pack in salt and ice for at least two hours. At serving time, dip the mold quickly into hot water, turn the pudding onto a cold platter, pour caramel sauce around the base, and serve at once.

This will serve twelve people.

MONTE CARLO PUDDING

* 1 quart of cream
* 6 ounces of sugar (⅔ of a cup)
* 4 tablespoons of creme de violette or violet liqueur
* ½ pound of candied violets
* 1 teaspoon of vanilla extract

Put half the cream over the heat in a double boiler. Pound or roll the violets, sift them, add the sugar and sufficient hot cream to dissolve them. Take the cream from the heat, add the violet sugar, and stir until it is dissolved; when cold, add the flavoring and the remaining cream. Freeze, and pack into a two quart pyramid mold; pack in salt and ice for at least two hours. At serving time, turn the ice onto a platter, garnish the base with whipped cream and the whole dessert with candied violets.

This will serve six to eight people.

MONTROSE PUDDING

* 1 quart of cream
* 1 cup of granulated sugar
* 1 tablespoon of vanilla extract
* 1 pint of Strawberry Water Ice
* Yolks of 6 eggs

Put half the cream over the heat in a double boiler. Beat the yolks and sugar together until light, add them to the boiling cream, and cook and stir for one minute until it begins to thicken. Remove from the heat, add the remaining pint of cream and the vanilla extract, and let stand until very cold.

Freeze, and pack into a round or melon mold, leaving a well in the center. Fill this well with Strawberry Water Ice (see recipe, page 68) that has been frozen for an hour before, and cover it with some of the pudding mixture that you have left in the freezer. Fasten the lid, bind the seam with a piece of muslin dipped in paraffin, and pack in salt and ice to stand for two to four hours. Serve with Montrose Sauce (see recipe, page 93) poured around it.

This will serve twelve people.

NESSELRODE PUDDING

* ❄ 1 pint of Spanish chestnuts
* ❄ ½ pound of sugar
* ❄ 1 pint of boiling water
* ❄ ⅔ cup of almond paste
* ❄ 1 pound of French candied fruit, mixed
* ❄ 1 pint of heavy cream
* ❄ ¼ pound of candied pineapple
* ❄ Yolks of six eggs
* ❄ 1 teaspoon of vanilla extract
* ❄ 4 tablespoons of sherry (optional)

Shell the chestnuts, scald and remove the brown skins, cover with boiling water and boil until they are tender, not too soft, and press them through a sieve. Cut the fruit into tiny pieces. Put the sugar and water in a saucepan, stir until the sugar is dissolved, wipe down the sides of the pan, and boil without stirring until the syrup forms a soft ball when dropped into ice water. Beat the yolks of the eggs until very light, add them to the boiling syrup, and stir over the heat until the mixture again boils. Remove from the heat and, with an ordinary eggbeater, whisk the mixture until it is cold and as thick as sponge cake batter. Add the fruit, chestnuts, almond paste, a teaspoon of vanilla extract and, if you use it, four tablespoons of sherry. Turn the mixture into the freezer, and, when it is frozen, stir in the cream whipped to a stiff froth. The mixture may now be repacked in the can, or it may be put into small molds or one large mold, and repacked for ripening.

If packed in a large mold, this will serve fifteen people; in the small molds or paper dessert cups, it will serve eighteen people.

NESSELRODE PUDDING, AMERICANA

* 1 small bottle, or sixteen preserved marrons*
* 1 quart of cream
* 4 ounces of sugar
* 4 tablespoons of sherry
* 1 tablespoon of vanilla extract
* Yolks of six eggs

Put half the cream in a double boiler over the heat; when hot, add the eggs and sugar beaten until light. Cook a minute, and cool. When cold, add one small bottle of marrons broken into quarters and the syrup from the bottle, the sherry, and vanilla extract. Freeze, stirring slowly. When frozen, stir in the remaining cream whipped to a stiff froth. Pack in small molds in salt and ice as directed. Freeze for at least 3 hours.

This will make twelve small molds.

---

*Preserved marrons are large chestnuts preserved in syrup.

ORANGE SOUFFLÉ

* ❋ 1 quart of cream
* ❋ 1 pint of orange juice
* ❋ ½ box of gelatin
* ❋ ¾ pound of sugar
* ❋ Yolks of six eggs

Cover the gelatin with a half cup of cold water and soak for a half hour. Add a half cup of boiling water, stir until the gelatin is dissolved, and add the sugar and the orange juice. Beat the yolks of the eggs until very light. Whip the cream. Add the uncooked yolks to the orange mixture, strain in the gelatin, stand the bowl in cold water and stir slowly until the mixture begins to thicken; carefully stir in the whipped cream, turn it in a mold or an ice cream freezer, pack with salt and ice, and let stand for three hours to freeze. This should not be frozen as hard as ice cream, and must not be stirred while freezing. Make sure, however, that the gelatin is thoroughly mixed with the other ingredients before putting the mixture into the freezer.

By changing the flavoring, using lemon in the place of orange, or a pint of strawberry juice, or a pint of raspberry and currant juice, an endless variety of soufflés may be made from this same recipe. These may be served plain, or with Montrose Sauce (see recipe, page 93).

This will serve twelve people.

PLOMBIERE

* ❊ 1 quart of cream
* ❊ ½ pound of Jordan almonds or ½ pound of almond paste
* ❊ ½ pound of sugar
* ❊ ½ pound of golden raisins
* ❊ Yolks of six eggs
* ❊ Apricot jam

Blanch the almonds and pound them to a paste, or use ½ pound of ordinary almond paste. Put half the cream in a double boiler over the heat, add the yolks and sugar beaten to a cream, add the almond paste. Stir until the mixture begins to thicken, remove from the heat and beat with an eggbeater for three minutes. Strain through a fine sieve, and, when very cold, add the raisins and the remaining cream. Freeze, turning the dasher very slowly at first and more rapidly toward the end. Remove the dasher, scrape down the sides of the can and pull the cream up, making a well in the center. Fill this well half full with apricot jam, cover over the pudding mixture, making it smooth; repack, and let stand for two hours.

Serve plain or with a cold puree of apricots.

This will serve twelve people.

ICED RICE PUDDING WITH A COMPOTE OF ORANGES

For the Pudding

* ½ cup of rice
* 1 quart of cream
* 1 pint of milk
* 2 teaspoons of vanilla extract or ½ vanilla bean
* ½ pound of sugar
* Yolks of six eggs

Rub the rice in a dry towel, and put it over the heat in a pint of cold water. Bring to a boil and boil twenty minutes; drain, add the milk and cook it in a double boiler for a half hour. While this is boiling, whip the cream to a stiff froth, and let stand in a cold place until needed. Press the rice through a fine sieve and return it to the double boiler. Beat the yolks of the eggs and the sugar until light, stir them into the hot rice, and stir and cook about two minutes, until the mixture begins to thicken.

Remove from the heat, add the vanilla extract, and let stand until very cold. When cold, freeze, turning the dasher rapidly toward the end. Remove the dasher, and stir in the whipped cream. Scrape down the sides of the can, and smooth the pudding. Put on the lid, fasten the hole in the top with a cork, cover the top with a piece of waxed paper, and pack with salt and ice. Let stand for at least two or three hours. Be very careful that the hole in the tub is open to prevent the salt water from overflowing the can.

For the Compote

* ❋ 1 dozen good quality oranges
* ❋ 1 pound of sugar
* ❋ ½ cup of water
* ❋ 1 teaspoon of lemon juice

Put the sugar and water over the heat to boil, wipe down the sides of the pan, skim the syrup, add the lemon juice, and boil until it spins a thread. Peel the oranges, cut them into halves crosswise, and with a sharp knife remove the cores. Dip one piece at a time into the hot syrup and place them on a platter to cool. Pour over any syrup that may be left.

This syrup must be thick, but not sufficiently thick to harden on the oranges.

To dish the pudding, lift the can from the ice, wipe it carefully on the outside, wrap the bottom of the mold in a towel dipped in boiling water, or hold it half an instant under cold water. Then, with a spatula loosen the pudding from the side of the can and shake it out into the center of a large round plate. Heap the oranges on top of the pudding, arranging them in a pyramid. Put the remaining quantity around the base of the pudding, pour over the syrup, and send to the table.

This pudding sounds elaborate and troublesome, but it is exceedingly palatable and one of the handsomest of all frozen dishes.

Using ice cream stem dishes, this will serve twenty-four people.

SULTANA (GOLDEN RAISIN) ROLL

* 1½ quarts of cream
* ½ pound of granulated sugar
* ½ cup of golden raisins
* 4 tablespoons of sherry
* 2 ounces of shelled pistachio nuts
* 1 teaspoon of almond extract
* 10 drops of green food coloring

Put one pint of cream and the sugar over the heat in a double boiler and stir until the sugar is dissolved. Remove from the heat, and, when cold, add a pint of the remaining cream. Chop the pistachio nuts very fine or put them through a food grinder, add them to the cream and add the flavoring and coloring, and freeze. Whip the remaining pint of cream to a stiff froth. Sprinkle the raisins with sherry and let them stand while you are freezing the pudding. When the pudding is frozen, remove the dasher and line an oval mold with the pistachio cream.

You may also use one-pound baking cans and line them to the depth of one inch.

Add the raisins to the whipped cream and stir in two tablespoons of powdered sugar. Fill the spaces in the cans with the whipped cream mixture, and put another layer of the pistachio cream over the top. Put on the lids, wrap each can in waxed paper, and put them down into coarse salt and ice, to freeze for at least two hours. At serving time, turn the puddings onto a long platter, fill the bottom of the platter with Claret Sauce (see recipe, page 91) or a strawberry sauce, and send to the table.

When cut into half-inch slices, this will serve twelve people.

SULTANA (GOLDEN RAISIN) PUDDING

* ❊ 1 pint of milk
* ❊ 1 pint of cream
* ❊ 6 ounces of sugar
* ❊ 1 cup of golden raisins
* ❊ 1 teaspoon of vanilla extract
* ❊ 4 tablespoons of sherry
* ❊ Yolks of 4 eggs

Put the milk in a double boiler, and, when hot, add the yolks and sugar beaten together; stir until this begins to thicken. Remove from the heat, add the vanilla extract, and, when cold, freeze it. Pour the sherry over the raisins. Garnish the bottom of a melon mold with the raisins, pack it in coarse ice and salt ready for the frozen pudding. Remove the dasher from the frozen mixture, and stir in the cream that has been whipped to a stiff froth. Add the remainder of the raisins, and pack at once into the mold; put on the lid and fasten as directed in other recipes.

This may be served plain or with whipped cream garnished with raisins.

This will serve eight people.

QUEEN PUDDING

Make a Strawberry Water Ice (see recipe, page 68) or use frozen strawberries. Pack a three-quart mold in a bucket or tub of ice and salt. Line the mold with the Strawberry Ice or frozen strawberries, fill the center with Tuttti Frutti (see recipe, page 51), using half the recipe; put on the lid, bind the seam, and let stand for at least two hours. When ready to serve, turn the pudding from the mold onto the center of a large round dish, garnish the base with whipped cream pressed through a star tube, and garnish the pudding with candied cherries. Here and there around the base of the whipped cream place a marron glacé.*

This will serve fifteen people.

....

ICE CREAM CROQUETTES

Mold vanilla ice cream with an ice cream scooper, roll them quickly in grated macaroons, and serve on a paper mat.

---

* A marron glacé is a confection consisting of a chestnut candied in sugar syrup and glazed.

THE MERRY WIDOW

Dish a pyramid of vanilla ice cream into an individual stem ice cream glass. Garnish the base of the ice cream with fresh strawberries, dust the cream thickly with toasted pine nuts, and baste the whole with four tablespoons of Claret Sauce (see recipe, page 91) flavored with two tablespoons of rum.

TUTTI FRUTTI PUDDING

* 1 pint of milk
* 1 pint of cream
* ½ pint of mixed candied fruits
* 4 eggs
* 1 cup of sugar
* 1 teaspoon of vanilla extract
* 2 tablespoons of sherry
* 1 tablespoon of brandy

Put the milk over the heat in a double boiler, add the yolks of the eggs and the sugar beaten together until light. When the mixture begins to thicken, remove from the heat and let stand until perfectly cold. Add all the flavorings. When the mixture is cold, add the cream, and partly freeze it; then add the fruit, and freeze to the right consistency. This should be packed at least two hours to ripen.

This will serve eight people.

TUTTI FRUTTI, ITALIAN FASHION

* ½ pound of sugar
* 1 pint of water
* 1 pint of cream
* ½ pint of chopped mixed candied fruits
* 1 teaspoon of vanilla extract
* 4 tablespoons of sherry
* Yolks of six eggs

Pour the sherry over the fruit. Beat the yolks until creamy. Put the sugar and water over the heat, stir until the sugar is dissolved, and boil five minutes; add the yolks of the eggs, beat until it again reaches the boiling point. Remove from the heat and beat until cold and thick. Add the cream, the fruit, and the vanilla extract. Freeze as directed on page vi.

This is usually served in small ice cream glasses garnished with whipped cream, or may be served plain. In the absence of ice cream glasses, use ordinary punch glasses.

This will fill ten glasses.

LALLA ROOKH

Fill a lemonade or ice cream glass ⅔ full of vanilla ice cream. Make a little well in the center and fill the space with rum and sherry mixed. Allow ⅔ of a tablespoon of rum and 1 tablespoon of sherry to each glass.

LILLIAN RUSSELL

Cut small, very cold cantaloupes into halves. Remove the seeds; fill the centers of the half melons with vanilla ice cream, and garnish with whipped cream pressed through a small star tube. Dish the halves on paper mats on a dessert plate, and send to the table.

....

PEACH MELBA

Dish a helping of vanilla ice cream in the center of a serving plate, place a whole brandied peach in the center of the ice cream, press it down into the ice cream, and baste four tablespoons of Claret Sauce (see recipe, page 91) over the top, and serve.

....

ARROWROOT CREAM

- ✳ 1 quart of milk
- ✳ 6 ounces of sugar
- ✳ 1 level tablespoon of arrowroot
- ✳ 2 teaspoons of vanilla extract

Moisten the arrowroot with a little cold milk; put the remaining milk in a double boiler; when hot, add the arrowroot and cook ten minutes; add the sugar. Remove from the heat and add the vanilla extract. When perfectly cold, freeze as directed on page vi.

This will serve six people.

ENGLISH APRICOT CREAM

* ½ pint of apricot jam
* 1 pint of cream
* ½ pint of milk
* 2 tablespoons of noyau or almond extract
* Juice of one lemon

Mix the jam and the cream, then carefully add the noyau or extract and the lemon juice. Press through a fine sieve, add the milk, and freeze as directed on page vi.

This will serve six people.

....

FROZEN CUSTARD

* 1 quart of milk
* 6 ounces of sugar
* 2 teaspoons of vanilla extract
* Yolks of four eggs
* Conserved fruit (optional)
* Chopped black walnuts (optional)

Put the milk in a double boiler, add the yolks of the eggs and the sugar beaten together, and stir until the mixture thickens. Remove from the heat, and, when cold, add the vanilla extract. Turn into the freezer and freeze as directed on page vi. A little chopped conserved fruit may be added after the dasher is removed. Chopped black walnuts may also be added.

This will serve six people.

FROZEN PLUM PUDDING

* 2 pint cans (32 oz. total) of condensed milk or 1 quart of whole milk
* ½ cup of seeded raisins
* ½ pound of sugar
* 24 almonds that have been blanched and chopped
* 2 ounces of shredded citron
* ¼ pound of candied cherries
* 2 teaspoons of vanilla extract
* 2 tablespoons of sherry
* ½ pint (8 oz.) of water
* Yolks of four eggs

Put milk in a double boiler over the heat, and stir until the milk is thoroughly heated; add the yolks of the eggs and the sugar beaten together, cook until it begins to thicken. Remove from the heat and strain. When cold, add the citron, raisins, the cherries cut into quarters, the almonds, vanilla extract, and sherry. When this is perfectly cold, freeze as directed on page vi. Do not repack or allow the mixture to stand in the freezer for more than a half hour.

Serve plain or with Montrose Sauce (see recipe, page 93).

This will serve twelve people.

GELATIN ICE CREAM

- 1 quart of milk
- ½ pint of cream
- 6 ounces of sugar
- 1 tablespoon of granulated gelatin
- 2 teaspoons of vanilla extract

Cover the gelatin with a little cold milk and let stand for fifteen minutes. Put the remaining milk in a double boiler; when scalding hot, add the sugar and the gelatin; stir until the sugar is dissolved. Remove from the heat, and, when perfectly cold, add the cream and the vanilla extract. Freeze as directed on page vi.

This will serve six people.

CHARLOTTE* GLACÉ

Make a quart of vanilla ice cream and stir a pint of cream whipped to a stiff froth into it. Line a charlotte cake pan with ladyfingers, fill it with the iced mixture, and place it at once in a can or bucket packed in salt and ice to freeze for one or two hours.

This will serve eight to twelve people.

---

* A charlotte cake is also known as an "icebox" cake.

MAPLE PANACHÉE

Fill stem ice cream dishes half full with caramel ice cream; put a layer of vanilla ice cream on top. Smooth it down and dust thickly with finely chopped toasted pecans.

A pint of each ice cream will fill six dishes.

GERMAN CHERRY BISCUITS

Fill paper dessert cups half full of Pineapple Water Ice (see recipe, page 66). Top with a layer of chopped candied cherries, then a layer of vanilla ice cream. Smooth it quickly, place a marron glacé in the center, and garnish the cream with a meringue made from the whites of two eggs and two tablespoons of powdered sugar. Dust this with grated macaroons, and send to the table.

Note: Make the meringue and grate the macaroons before dishing the ice cream.

A pint of each cream will fill eight dessert cups..

FRUIT SALAD, ICED

Make one quart of Lemon Water Ice (see recipe, page 64) or Orange Water Ice (see recipe, page 66) and let stand for at least one or two hours to ripen. Make a fruit salad from stemmed strawberries, sliced bananas cut into tiny bits, a few very ripe cherries, a grated pineapple, and the pulp of four or five oranges. After the water ice is frozen rather hard, pack it in a border mold, put on the lid or cover, bind the seam with a strip of muslin dipped in paraffin, and repack to freeze for three or four hours. Sweeten the fruit combination, if you would like, by adding a tablespoon or two of brandy and sherry, and stand this on the ice until very cold. At serving time, turn the mold of water ice onto a round compote dish, quickly fill the center with fruit salad, garnish the outside with fresh roses or violets, and send at once to the table.

This will serve eight to ten people.

COUPE ST. JACQUE

Make a fruit salad as in preceding recipe. Make a pint of Orange Water Ice (see recipe, page 66) or Strawberry Water Ice (see recipe, page 68). At serving time, fill parfait or ice cream glasses half full with the fruit salad; fill the remaining half with water ice, smooth it over, garnish the top with whipped cream, put a maraschino cherry in the center, and serve. Other fruits may be used for the salad.

This will fill twelve parfait glasses.

Water Ices and Sherbets or Sorbets

A water ice is a mixture of water, fruit, and sugar, frozen without much stirring; in fact, a water ice can be made in an ordinary tin kettle packed in a bucket. If an ice cream freezer is used, the stirring should be done occasionally. Personally, I prefer to pack the can, put on the lid and fasten the hole with a cork rather than to use the dasher, stirring now and then with a paddle. If you use the crank, turn slowly for a few minutes, then allow the mixture to stand for five minutes; turn slowly again, and again rest, and continue this until the water ice is frozen. A much longer time is required for freezing water ice than ice cream.

When the mixture is thoroughly frozen, take out the dasher, scrape down the sides of the can, and give the ice a thorough beating with a wooden spoon. Put the cork in the lid of the can, draw the water from the tub, repack it with coarse ice and salt, cover it with paper and a piece of burlap, and let stand for two or three hours to ripen just as you would ice cream.

When it is necessary to make water ice every day or two, it is best to make a syrup and stand it aside ready for use.

Fruit jellies may be used in the place of fresh fruits, allowing one pint of jelly, the juice of one lemon, and a half pound of sugar to each quart of water.

When water ice is correctly frozen, it has the appearance of hard wet snow. It must not be frothy or light.

A sherbet or sorbet is made from the same mixture as a water ice, stirred constantly while it is freezing, and has a meringue, made from the white of one egg and a tablespoon of powdered sugar, stirred in after the dasher is removed.

APPLE WATER ICE

- ❊ 1 pound of tart apples
- ❊ 1 cup of sugar
- ❊ 1 pint of water
- ❊ Juice of one lemon or lime

Quarter and core the apples, but do not pare them. Slice them, add the water, cover and stew until tender, about five minutes. Press through a sieve, add the sugar and lemon juice. When cold, freeze as directed on page 60. Serve in lemonade glasses at dinner with roasted duck, goose, or pork.

This will serve six people.

APRICOT WATER ICE

- ❊ 1 quart can of apricots
- ❊ ½ cup of sugar
- ❊ 1 pint of water
- ❊ Juice of one lemon

Press the apricots through a sieve, add all the other ingredients, and freeze as directed on page 60. Serve in lemonade glasses for afternoon tea. Pass sweet wafers.

This will serve eight people.

CHERRY WATER ICE

* ❋ 2 full quarts of sour cherries
* ❋ 1 pound of sugar
* ❋ 1 quart of water
* ❋ 2 drops of bitters (optional)

Stew the cherries in the water for ten minutes and press through a sieve; add the sugar, and, if you have it, two drops of bitters. When cold, freeze as directed on page 60.

This will serve ten people.

....

CURRANT WATER ICE

* ❋ 1 pint of currant juice
* ❋ 1 pound of sugar
* ❋ 1 pint of boiling water

Add the sugar to the water, and stir over the heat until it is dissolved. Boil five minutes. Remove from the heat; when cool, add the currant juice. When cold, freeze as directed on page 60.

This will serve six people.

CURRANT AND RASPBERRY WATER ICE

- ❄ 1 pint of currant juice
- ❄ 1 pint of raspberry juice
- ❄ 1 pint of water
- ❄ ¾ pound of sugar

Add the sugar to the water, stir until boiling, boil five minutes, and, when cool, add the raspberry and currant juices, and freeze as directed on page 60.

Using punch glasses, this will serve eight people.

GRAPE WATER ICE

- ❄ 1 pint of grape juice
- ❄ 1 quart of water
- ❄ 1 pound of sugar
- ❄ Juice of one lemon

Boil the sugar and water together for five minutes. Remove from the heat, add the lemon juice, and skim. When cold, add the grape juice, and freeze as directed on page 60.

If fresh grapes are to be used, select Muscatels or Concords. Pulp the grapes, boil the pulps, press them through a sieve, and add the skins and the pulps to the sugar and water. Boil five minutes, press as much as possible through a sieve, and freeze.

This will serve eight people.

LEMON WATER ICE

* 4 large lemons
* 1 quart of water
* 1¼ pounds of sugar

Grate the rinds of two lemons into the sugar, add the water, stir over the heat until the sugar is dissolved, and boil for five minutes. Strain and let stand to cool. When cold, add the juice of the lemons, and freeze as directed on page 60.

This will serve six people.

....

GINGER WATER ICE

* 6 ounces of crystallized ginger
* 4 lemons
* 1 quart of water
* 1 pound of sugar

Put four ounces of the ginger through an ordinary food grinder and cut the remaining two ounces into fine bits. Boil the sugar and water together for five minutes and add the lemon juice and ground ginger. Remove from the heat, add the bits of ginger, and, when cold, freeze as directed on page 60. Ginger Water Ice is better when left to stand for two hours after it is frozen. Nice to serve with roasted or braised beef.

Using small punch glasses, this will serve eight people.

MILLE FRUIT WATER ICE

* ½ pint of grape juice
* 6 lemons
* 1 orange
* 4 tablespoons of sherry
* ½ pound of preserved cherries or pineapple, or both, mixed
* 1½ pounds of sugar
* 1 quart of water

Grate the yellow rind of the orange and the rind of one lemon into the sugar, add the water, stir over the heat until the sugar is dissolved, boil five minutes, and strain. Add the fruit cut into small pieces, the juice of the orange and the lemons; when cold, add the grape juice and sherry, and freeze, using the dasher. Do not stir rapidly, but stir continuously, as slowly as possible. When the mixture is frozen, remove the dasher and repack the can; ripen at least two hours.

This is one of the nicest of all the water ices, and may be served on top of Coupe St. Jacque (see recipe, page 58), or at dinner in sherbet glasses with roasted veal or beef.

This will serve ten people.

ORANGE WATER ICE

* 12 large oranges
* 1 pound of sugar
* 1 quart of water

Grate the yellow rinds from three oranges into the sugar, add the water, boil five minutes, and strain; when cold, add the juice of the oranges, and freeze as directed on page 60.

This will serve ten people.

PINEAPPLE WATER ICE

* 2 ripe pineapples or 1 quart can of crushed pineapple
* 1 quart of water
* 1½ pounds of sugar
* Juice of 2 lemons

Pare the pineapples, remove the eyes, and grate the fruit into the water. Add the sugar and lemon juice, boil five minutes, and, when cold, freeze as directed on page 60.

This will serve ten people.

POMEGRANATE WATER ICE

- ❄ 12 pomegranates
- ❄ 1 pint of cold water
- ❄ 1 pound of sugar

Cut the pomegranates into halves, remove the seeds carefully from the inside bitter skin; press them with a potato masher in the colander, allowing the juice to run through into a bowl; be careful not to mash the seeds. Add the sugar to the juice and stir until it is dissolved; then add cold water, and freeze as directed on page 60. This is very nice to serve with a meat course, and also nice for the garnish of a fruit salad.

This will serve six people.

....

RASPBERRY WATER ICE

- ❄ 1 quart of red raspberries
- ❄ 1 pound of sugar
- ❄ 1 quart of water
- ❄ Juice of two lemons

Add the sugar and the lemon juice to the raspberries, stir and let stand for one hour. Press through a sieve, add the water, and freeze as directed on page 60.

This will serve eight people.

ROMAN PUNCH

Make one quart of Lemon Water Ice (see recipe, page 64). When ready to serve, pour into small punch glasses, make a little well in the center, and fill the space with Jamaican rum.

This will serve eight people.

....

SOURSOP SHERBET OR ICE

Squeeze the juice from one large soursop, strain, and add four tablespoons of sugar, boiled a moment with four tablespoons of water. Freeze as directed on page 60.

When frozen, a quart of soursop will serve six people.

....

STRAWBERRY WATER ICE

* 1 quart of strawberries
* 1 pound of sugar
* 1 quart of water
* Juice of 2 lemons

Add the sugar and the lemon juice to the stemmed strawberries, let them stand one hour; mash them through a colander, and then, if you would like, strain through a fine sieve. Add the water, and freeze as directed on page 60.

This will serve eight people.

CRANBERRY SHERBET

* ❊ 1 pint of cranberries
* ❊ ½ pound of sugar
* ❊ ½ pint of water

Add the water to the cranberries, cover, bring to a boil; press through a colander, return them to the heat, add the sugar, and stir until the sugar dissolves. Remove from the heat, and, when cold, freeze, stirring slowly the whole time. Serve with the main course at dinner.

This will serve eight people.

CUCUMBER SORBET

* ❊ 2 large cucumbers
* ❊ 2 tart apples
* ❊ 1 pint of water
* ❊ 1 teaspoon of sugar
* ❊ ½ teaspoon of salt
* ❊ 1 tablespoon of gelatin
* ❊ ¼ teaspoon of black pepper
* ❊ Juice of one lemon

Peel the cucumbers, cut them into halves, and remove the seeds. Dissolve the gelatin in a half cup of hot water. Grate the flesh of the cucumbers; grate the apples, add them to the cucumbers, and add all the other ingredients. Freeze as you would ordinary sherbet.

Serve in tiny glasses; perfect with cod or halibut.

This will fill eight small stem glasses.

GOOSEBERRY SORBET

* ½ pint of gooseberry jam
* 4 tablespoons of sugar
* 1 pint of water
* Juice of one lemon

Mix all the ingredients together and freeze, turning slowly the entire time. Serve in small glasses. This is usually served at Christmas dinner with goose.

This will serve six people.

MINT SHERBET

* 2 dozen stalks of spearmint
* ½ pound of sugar
* 1 quart of water
* Juice of 3 lemons

Strip the leaves from the stalks of the mint, chop them to a pulp, and rub them with the sugar. Add the water, bring to a boil, boil five minutes, and, when cold, add three drops of green food coloring and the juice of the lemons; strain and freeze, turning slowly the entire time.

Serve at dinner with mutton or lamb.

When using small stem glasses, this will serve eight people.

ORANGE SHERBET

* 1 pint of orange juice
* Grated rinds of 2 oranges
* 2 tablespoons of gelatin
* ¾ pound of sugar
* 1 pint of water

Cover the gelatin with an extra half cup of cold water and soak for a half hour. Add the sugar to the pint of water and stir it over the heat until it boils; add the grated rinds of two oranges and the juice; strain through a fine sieve and freeze, turning the freezer slowly the whole time. Remove the dasher, stir in a meringue made from the white of one egg, and repack to ripen for at least an hour.

This will serve six people.

TOMATO SORBET OR SHERBET

* 1 quart can or 12 fresh tomatoes
* 1 slice of onion
* 1 blade of mace (available at gourmet or specialty spice shops)
* ¼ teaspoon of celery seed
* 1 pint of water
* 1 teaspoon of salt
* 1 teaspoon of paprika
* 1 tablespoon of gelatin
* Juice of one lemon
* A dash of cayenne

Add all the ingredients to the tomatoes, stir over the heat until the mixture reaches the boiling point, boil five minutes and strain through a fine sieve. When this is cold, freeze according to the rule for sherbets, turning slowly the entire time.

Serve in punch glasses at dinner as an accompaniment to roast beef, or venison, or a saddle of mutton.

If fresh tomatoes are used, simply cut them into halves and cook them without peeling.

This will fill nine or ten punch glasses.

Frozen
Fruits

....

Frozen fruits are mixed and frozen the same as water ices, that is, they are only stirred occasionally while freezing, but the fruit must be mashed or it will form little balls of ice through a partly frozen mixture. The only difference between a water ice and a frozen fruit is that the mixture is not strained, and more fruit and less water is used. If canned fruits are used, and these recipes followed, reduce the amount of sugar. Cream may be used in place of water with sub-acid fruits.

....

FROZEN APRICOTS

* ❋ 1 quart of apricots
* ❋ 2 tablespoons of gelatin
* ❋ 1 cup of sugar
* ❋ 1 pint of cream

Drain the apricots from the can, mash them through a colander, add the sugar and stir until the sugar is dissolved. Cover the gelatin with a half cup of cold water and soak for a half hour. Stand it over hot water, stir until dissolved, add it to the apricot mixture, and freeze. When frozen, remove the dasher and stir in the cream whipped to a stiff froth.

Repack and let stand two hours to ripen.

This will serve ten people.

....

FROZEN BANANAS

* ❋ 12 large ripe bananas
* ❋ 1 pound of sugar
* ❋ ½ pint of water
* ❋ 1 pint of cream
* ❋ Juice of 2 lemons

Peel the bananas and mash them through a colander. Add the sugar to the water, and boil five minutes; when cold, add the lemon juice and the bananas. Put the mixture into a freezing can, stir slowly until frozen. Remove the dasher and carefully stir in the cream whipped to a stiff froth.

This will serve ten to twelve people.

FROZEN CHOCOLATE

* ❉ 1 quart of milk
* ❉ 3 ounces of chocolate
* ❉ ⅔ cup of sugar
* ❉ 1 pint of water
* ❉ ½ pint of cream, whipped
* ❉ 1 teaspoon of vanilla extract

Grate the chocolate and put it in a double boiler with the water and sugar; let the water in the surrounding boiler boil fifteen minutes, beat well, and add the milk. Stir until thoroughly mixed and the milk is very hot. Remove from the heat, add the vanilla extract, and when the mixture is cold, freeze, turning slowly the entire time. Serve in chocolate cups with the whipped cream on top.

This will fill nine chocolate cups.

FROZEN PINEAPPLE

* ❉ 2 large pineapples
* ❉ 1 quart of water
* ❉ 1 pound of sugar
* ❉ Juice of one lemon

Peel the pineapples and grate them. Add the sugar to the water, stir until the sugar is dissolved, boil five minutes and cool; add the pineapple and lemon juice, and freeze, turning the freezer slowly.

This will serve eight to ten people.

FROZEN COFFEE

* ❈ 1 quart of cold water
* ❈ ½ pound of sugar
* ❈ 6 heaping tablespoons of finely ground coffee
* ❈ ½ pint of cream

Put the coffee and the water in a double boiler over the heat and let the water in the bottom pot boil for at least twenty minutes after boiling begins. Strain through two thicknesses of cheesecloth, add the sugar, stir until the sugar is dissolved, and let stand until very cold. Add the cream and the unbeaten white of one egg. Freeze, turning the freezer slowly. This should be the consistency of a soft mush and very light.

Serve in coffee cups, either plain or with whipped cream on top.

This will serve six people.

FROZEN RASPBERRIES

* ❈ 1 quart of raspberries
* ❈ ¾ pound of sugar
* ❈ 1 pint of water
* ❈ Juice of one lemon

Add the sugar and the lemon juice to the berries, mash them with a potato masher. Let them stand one hour, add the water, and freeze.

This will serve eight people.

FROZEN PEACHES, NO. 1

* 2 pounds of very ripe peaches
* 6 peach kernels
* 1 pint of water
* ½ pound of sugar
* Juice of one lemon

Crack the kernels, chop them fine, add them to the sugar, add the water, and boil five minutes; strain and let stand to cool. Pare the peaches, press them through a colander, add them to the cold syrup, turn into the freezer, and stir slowly until the mixture is frozen. If the peaches are colorless, add a few drops of peach/orange food coloring before freezing.

This will serve eight people.

FROZEN PEACHES, NO. 2

* 1 quart of peach pulp
* 1 pint of cream
* ¾ pound of sugar
* Juice of one lemon

Add the lemon juice to the peach pulp, add the sugar, and let stand, stirring every now and then until the sugar is dissolved. Freeze the mixture, stirring slowly; when frozen, remove the dasher, and fold in the cream whipped to a stiff froth.

This is one of the nicest ices for a light afternoon or evening informal meal.

Using stem glasses, this will serve ten people.

FROZEN WATERMELON

Scrape the center from a very ripe watermelon, chop quickly and press through a colander. To each pint of this juice, add a half cup of sugar and four tablespoons of sherry. Freeze until it is like wet snow. Serve in stem glasses.

One pint will fill three stem glasses.

....

FROZEN STRAWBERRIES

* 1 quart of very ripe strawberries
* 1 pound of sugar
* 1 pint of water
* Juice of one lemon

Add the sugar and lemon juice to the berries, let them stand one hour. Mash the berries through a colander, add the water, and freeze, turning the dasher constantly but very slowly.

This will serve eight people.

Frappés
*
Parfaits
*
Mousses

A frappé is nothing more than a water ice partly frozen. For instance, Cafe Frappé is a partly frozen coffee. The mixture looks like wet snow. A Champagne Frappé is champagne packed in salt and ice and the bottles shaken until the champagne is partly frozen.

A parfait is a dessert made from frozen whipped cream, sweetened and flavored. An old-fashioned parfait was not frozen in an ice cream freezer; the mixture was packed at once into a mold, and the mold packed in salt and ice to freeze for two or three hours. To be perfect, the mixture must be frozen on the outside to the depth of one and a half to two inches, with a soft center. The quick parfait given under Frozen Puddings and Desserts (see page 38) is now in general use.

A mousse is a parfait frozen to the center. This mixture is not smooth like ice cream, but is frozen in crystals. When made correctly, a mousse should have a moss-like texture when cut.

BURNT ALMOND MOUSSE

* ¼ pound of Jordan almonds
* 2 ounces of almond paste
* ⅔ cup of powdered sugar
* 1 pint of thick cream
* 1 teaspoon of almond extract

Whip the cream to a very stiff froth. Blanch, toast, and grind the almonds, putting them through an ordinary food grinder; rub them with the almond paste, adding the extract and about two tablespoons of water or sherry.

Sprinkle the sugar over the whipped cream, and then fold in the nut mixture. Pack at once into a mold, put on the lid, fasten the seam with a strip of muslin dipped in paraffin and pack in coarse salt and ice to freeze for two to three hours.

Serve plain or dusted with chopped almonds.

This will serve six people.

COFFEE MOUSSE

* 1 pint of cream
* ½ cup of powdered sugar
* 2 tablespoons of coffee extract

Whip the cream to a stiff froth, sprinkle over the sugar, add the coffee extract, and, when well mixed, pack and freeze.

This will serve six people.

DUCHESS MOUSSE

4 eggs, separated

½ cup of sugar

1 pint of cream

1 teaspoon of vanilla extract

5 drops of red food coloring

Beat the yolks of the eggs and the sugar until very, very light; fold in the whites of the eggs and the vanilla extract. Stand the bowl in a pan of boiling water and beat continuously until the ingredients are hot; remove from the heat and beat constantly for ten minutes. When this is cool, fold in the cream whipped to a stiff froth, pack and freeze.

Serve with quince jelly poured over the mousse.

This will serve eight people.

EGYPTIAN MOUSSE

- ½ cup of rice
- 1 tablespoon of gelatin
- ⅔ cup of sugar
- ¼ pound of dates, chopped
- ½ pint of milk
- 1 pint of cream
- 1 teaspoon of vanilla extract

Rinse the rice and cook as directed. Drain, add the milk, and cook in a double boiler 15 minutes. Add the sugar, the gelatin that has been moistened in cold water, and the chopped dates. Remove from the heat, add the vanilla extract, and when the mixture is cold, carefully fold in the whipped cream. Freeze as directed in a mold, and serve with cold quince jelly sauce.

This will serve ten people.

PISTACHIO MOUSSE

* ❋ 4 ounces of pistachio nuts
* ❋ 1 tablespoon of gelatin
* ❋ 1 pint of water
* ❋ 1 pint of cream
* ❋ ½ pound of sugar
* ❋ 1 teaspoon of almond extract
* ❋ 3 drops of green food coloring

Blanch the pistachio nuts and put them through a food grinder. Boil the sugar and water for five minutes; when cool, add the food coloring, the pistachio nuts, and the gelatin moistened in a little cold water. When this is cold, fold in the cream beaten to a stiff froth, and freeze in a mold as directed.

If this is not too well mixed, the cream will separate, which makes for a more attractive dessert. When the mousse is turned from the mold it will then have a solid white base with a rather green, beautiful transparent mixture at the top.

This will serve ten people.

RICE MOUSSE WITH A COMPOTE OF MANDARINS

* ½ cup of rice
* 1 tablespoon of gelatin
* ⅔ cup of sugar
* 1 pint of milk
* 1 pint of cream
* ¼ pound of candied cherries
* 1 teaspoon of vanilla extract

Wash and boil the rice in water for twenty minutes, drain, put it in a double boiler with the milk and sugar; stir until the sugar is dissolved, cover the kettle and cook slowly for twenty minutes. Press through a sieve, add the vanilla extract, and the gelatin covered with cold water. When this is cold, fold in the cream whipped to a stiff froth; pack and freeze.

This is best frozen in an ordinary ice cream can; simply remove the dasher, put in the mixture and pack it to freeze for two or three hours.

While this is ripening, separate the mandarins into sections. Boil together, for five minutes, one pound of sugar, a half pint of water, and the juice of one lemon. Remove from the heat, add the mandarin sections at once, stir lightly until they are thoroughly covered with the syrup, and let stand until very cold.

At serving time, wipe the outside of the freezing can with a warm towel, turn the mousse into the center of a round dish, heap the mandarin sections around the base and over the top in the form of a pyramid, pour over the syrup, and send at once to the table.

This will serve twelve people.

Sauces for Ice Creams

CLARET SAUCE

Boil one cup of sugar and a half cup of water with ¼ teaspoon of cream of tartar for five minutes. Remove from the heat, add one cup of claret*, and let stand until icy cold.

....

HOT CHOCOLATE SAUCE

* ½ cup of cream or condensed milk
* 2 ounces of chocolate
* 1 cup of sugar
* 1 teaspoon of vanilla extract

Put all the ingredients into a saucepan and stir over the heat until they reach a boiling point; boil until the mixture slightly hardens when dropped into cold water. Add the vanilla extract, turn at once into a sauceboat and send to the table. This must be sufficiently thin to dip nicely over the ice cream.

---

* Claret is a red table wine produced in the Bordeaux region of France.

MAPLE SAUCE

* 1 cup of sugar
* 1 teaspoon of lemon juice
* 1 cup of water
* 1 teaspoon of maple flavoring or extract

Put half the sugar into an iron saucepan and let stand over the heat until it melts and browns. Quickly add the water, the remaining sugar, and the lemon juice, and boil for about two minutes. Remove from the heat and add the flavoring. This may be served plain, or with chopped fruits or nuts.

NUT SAUCE

* 1 cup of sugar
* ½ cup of chopped nuts
* 1 cup of water
* 1 teaspoon of caramel
* 2 teaspoons of sherry
* ¼ teaspoon cream of tartar or 1 teaspoon of lemon juice

Boil the sugar and water with the cream of tartar or the lemon juice for five minutes. Remove from the heat and add all the other ingredients, and let stand to cool.

MONTROSE SAUCE

* ½ tablespoon of granulated gelatin
* ¼ cup of sugar
* ½ cup of milk
* 1 pint of cream
* 2 tablespoons of brandy
* 4 tablespoons of sherry (optional)
* 1 teaspoon of vanilla extract
* Yolks of 3 eggs

Cover the gelatin with milk, let it soak a half hour, and put it, with the milk, in a double boiler over the heat. Beat the yolks of the eggs and the sugar together, add them to the hot milk, stir about one minute until the mixture begins to thicken. Remove from the heat and, when cold, add the vanilla extract and the brandy and, if you would like, four tablespoons of sherry.

Let stand until very, very cold.

ORANGE SAUCE

* ½ pint of orange juice
* ½ pint of water
* ½ cup of sugar
* 1 tablespoon of arrowroot
* Whites of three eggs

Add the sugar to the water, and, when boiling hot, add the arrowroot moistened with water. Beat the whites of the eggs to a stiff froth; gradually add the hot mixture, beating continuously. Add the orange juice, beat again. Pour it into a sauceboat and let stand until very cold.

....

WALNUT SAUCE

Melt maple sugar with a little water, and to each cup of syrup add a half cup of chopped black walnuts. Maple syrup may also be used by adding half the quantity of boiling water and the nuts.

Index

INDEX